# CONTENTS

# The Uses Of Litteracy: a new voice from Coventry

I wish here to forestall some of the more obvious criticisms that may be levelled at this volume. They have already been made in reaction to the printed (though not the performance) poems: feedback Jackie Smallridge received when she sent work to a 'Literature Reading Service' run by the Arts Council in Birmingham. Writing with her "editor's hat on", their expert – let us anonymise her name to 'Raw Egghard' – states:

> People write poetry for many different reasons: to make sense of their own experience, to get something off their chest, to raise awareness of a situation or perhaps to use language and imagery to translate an everyday experience into something which will have wider resonance for the reader. I suspect, from reading your work, you a) want to get something off your chest and b) you wish to raise awareness of a situation, though I'm not sure whether you are writing for your own pleasure or whether you wish your poetry to reach a wider audience. If you are writing for the reasons above and you don't want publication or wider recognition, then you might just as well carry on producing writing such as you have submitted, as no one else will see it. However, given that you have submitted your work for assessment, I suspect that you wish to reach a wider audience, so I am going to make some points about how you can improve your writing.
>
> Currently, the language you use in your work is crude, that is to say the work is littered with obscenities which have no place in contemporary poetry. An obscenity is never a substitute for a well thought out image or feeling. Do get hold of a few contemporary poetry collections and look at how poets use language, this will help you to refine your own.

Raw Egghard goes on to express specific dislike for certain of these crude, obscene, unpoetic words:

> You seem to be writing in the persona of 'Scrubber Jack', indeed, lots of poets use voices and personas, however, you have adopted a persona which has a repetitive and it has to be said,

offensive, voice. Using words like, 'Pikey', 'Banana-Man', and 'Nigger' is both unacceptable and panders to crude racial and social stereotypes. If you want to write about people, make them come alive, make them real by allowing us to see them as individuals.

Some counter-arguments. Firstly 'Scrubber Jack' is not exactly a persona; more accurately she is a character developed by Jackie Smallridge for 'performance poetry' readings. In fact, there are many different personae in the volume – some of the voices being so obviously male should have given a hint of this. Next, aside from Egghard's wonky grammar, which seems to suggest you can pander to crude racial and social stereotypes and yet be acceptable, just by avoiding certain taboo words (perhaps she did hit the nail on the head, but it looks like an accident) – aside from this, her argument is simple, even inane: rude words are bad, polite words are good and Jackie, user of bad words, is some simplistic British National Party racist. It is hoped that this volume contains something altogether darker, where the only alive, real, individual people turn out to be the speakers of each poem (the twists of perspective in poems such as 'Dipping Their Wick', 'Annoying Shit', 'The Whore' and 'Winding Her Up' will give a better idea of the technique). In factual terms, Egghard is plain wrong about audience, for Jackie's work, unvarnished as it may be, is increasingly in demand in West Midlands literary circles, and in the local press. And as for "obscenity", I have always found Dreadlock Alien's summary of Philip Larkin apt (I paraphrase…):

Then I hear 'bout a man name Larkin
Who write lots of poetry:
He say rude things 'bout his Mum and Dad
While working in a library.

If Larkin isn't contemporary enough for Egghard, she could try a dose of her fellow-Brummie, Matt Nunn. But her preferences – "Carol Ann Duffy, Jean Sprackland, Paul

Farley" – reveal her own prejudices more strongly than they illuminate what she thinks of as the murky world of a Scrubber's poetry: prejudices towards the literate, the safe, the mainstream and a tipping away from writing that has no truck with "the pretence that life, give or take a few social distinctions, is the same as ever, that gentility, decency and all the other social totems will eventually muddle through" (the words of Al Alvarez, in his famous 1962 essay 'The New Poetry, or Beyond the Gentility Principle'). Rough and rootsy, like the dub poetry first published in *Savacou* 3/4 (1970), which protested a Jamaica fraught by poverty and postcolonial disillusionment, Jackie Smallridge's verse cries foul at the treatment of, and asserts her right to represent, the chavs and slags of twenty-first century Britain.

Doris a modder of four
get a wuk as a domestic
Boss man move een
an bap si kaisico she pregnant again
bap si kaisico she pregnant again
an me cyaan believe it
me seh me cyaan believe it
(Mikey Smith, 'Me Cyaaann Believe It')

It will be objected that realism moves away from literature, towards sociology, documentary; that to imagine is more difficult than to live; yet such a view is probably untenable below a certain level of privilege, and anyway imagination must surely involve empathy. Violence, deprivation, drug abuse, teenage sexuality and, yes, low literacy levels – these are problems that poets, language's workers, can assist in tackling.

But of course these are different conceptions of editing as much as of poetry. Jackie gave me over two hundred poems, and yes, they were raw, gutsy, at times uneven. The answer seemed to be not to deny her worldview, to moralise and sermonise and in the end refuse to engage with writing from that world. Instead, it was a case of looking at what was interesting in the poems, and through helping Jackie tighten up the metric while seeking to retain her natural cadence, by helping her legitimise their central logic while retaining the dialect edge, amplify the songlike qualities of her voice and clarify her ideas. The results are at times unsettling, and often earthily comical (classic English trait, from Chaucer onwards): for these are COV dialect poems, perhaps in some cases full songs, with a strange and, to my ears, unusual melody – the register as well as the vocab are how language is spoken in the social clubs and housing estates of this city. Grim, stoical, bawdy, tender by turns, it is poetry in the common speech of West Midlands people. There are even love-songs to cars: local *leitmotiv*.

Since a main linguistic resource of *Scrubberjack* is language of a particularly demotic and heightened nature, where neologisms and oaths wrestle for space, where cartoonish characters indulge obscene and violent fantasies, may it not be a species of contemporary literature? I do not believe it will damage the Heaventree imprint to publish the occasional poem in the oral tradition from a writer who has something new to say, and I don't believe (the inference is there) that Jackie Smallridge is incapable of improving her poetry, that encouragement, investment, opportunity are a waste of time. I look forward to Jackie's second collection – where she moves beyond rhyme and continues to push at the oddly shocking boundary she has identified where poetry starts to sound like something poets say isn't.

Jonathan Morley
Coventry, August 2007

## Acknowledgements

My thanks to all my friends and colleagues from Building 523 at Jaguar Land Rover, Gaydon, especially Lorna Macauley; and also to Chris, for being at my side. To my husband Adrian and my family, and to all the people I've met who have taken me under their wing over the last year: Matt Nunn, Richard Wood, Jo Roberts, Marc Williams, Sean Kelly, Rotunda Publishing, Ravinder Dhaliwal for the pictures, Jen, Kate and Sarah, Rachel Flint, all the Heaventree poets and Mr. Morley himself. Thanks for having faith in me.

## Airs And Graces

The people I've lived with all my life
Are people you might call lowlife
They don't have any airs and graces
And they can get in people's faces

What you see is what you get
They've done things they regret
But deep down they have hearts of gold
And stories to be told

It's not all made-up stuff
And it's written very rough
People like the nitty-gritty
It's wrong to make it pretty

It doesn't come into any category
Some people write like you and some like me

# Part I

## Dipping Their Wick

You don't have to get hitched
To a two-timing bitch
Don't take her for your bride
Just use her for a ride

She does the dirty on you
Been with half your crew
Dipping their wick
Think you're fucking thick

You're working at the track
She shags behind your back
Nothing special you know
Penny a throw

She's clatty as fuck
Always been bad luck
Get it in your head
Don't take her in your bed

Get your life back
Come with us on the crack
Fat birds and thin ones too
To satisfy you

## Do Us A Deal

Hey mate, do us a deal on a car
I fancy the new Jaguar

The one they're all talking about
The one that goes flat out

The one that catches your eye
Go on giz a try.

It's a mean machine
It's pristine and clean

It's smooth and suave
It's the king of cars

Come on do us a deal
I want one – for real.

## Black And Blue

I bet you've never watched your kin
Sitting sticking the needle in,
I bet you've never tried to suffer their pain
And known what it's like: it drives you insane.

I bet you've never watched them puke
And wondered if today's a fluke
When tomorrow comes round so fast
You don't know how long they'll last.

Have you seen their eyes so red
And watched when they can't get to bed?
Have you seen them go to skin and bone
And watched them sit all day at the phone,

Sitting waiting for their next fix
And scaring you out of your wits?
Are you sick of them coming in black and blue?
It's surprising what their mates will do.

No one wants to have mates like that,
A punch and a blow to the head with a bat:
My eyes fill up, my tears do flow
For it's off to court again I'll go.

It's not a good example to give to your brother,
Your sister and to me, your mother:
Once again I'll be at your side
Knowing to the judge that you lied.

You go against all my beliefs
Hanging round with druggies and thieves
And as a mother what can I do
When you know that I'll be there for you?

## Uncle Fester

I've had to lay low for a while,
They're calling me a paedophile.
I'm the one who got tagged
Shagging a fourteen-year-old slag.

She gave evidence to the police
When I shot my load on her fleece;
We're seventeen-year-old lads,
Don't care where we empty our bags.

My mates won't stand by me,
The bastards go and flee,
They don't want the attention,
Scared names will get mentioned.

I know I can't win the case
In this trial I have to face
And live with forever;
Have to pull myself together.

I'll be known as Uncle Fester,
You know, the child molester.
But it's the way it has to be,
The fucking bitch has hung me.

## Runny Eggs

I've got a problem, see
Involves me willy and me
I know it's a bit absurd
Involves me and me bird

We get to the good bit
All I can say is "Shit!"
Like having runny eggs
Down there inside me kecks

Common problem I've got
Me skids are full of snot
I wear jeans all the time
Me kecks are full of slime

Am I the only bloke
With trousers full of yolk?
I'm going to see the doc
Get treatment for me cock

If he gives me a cure
I'll be a stud for sure.

## Big Massive Woman

She's my big massive woman I adore,
She makes people's mouths drop to the floor,
She's smooth and black and shiny and bright
And I like to flash her around at night.
I never put me foot down, not too much
Cos she'd make such a noise, she likes a gentle touch;
She's got everything, all mod cons
Including some extra special ones!
I know I'll have to trade her in one day:
How can anyone give their BMW away?

## Men

I'm your resident jobey chopper,
And I try to do my job proper.
Just cos you wear suits so neat
Don't give you permission to shit my seat.

You men in the office take the piss,
The urinals you often miss.
Pissing contests you must have:
Can't you just use the bloody lav?

Sticky substance on my floor,
Best kept behind the bedroom door,
Pubic hair everywhere –
It isn't fair to your jobey chopper.

I want everyone to know
Just how far men will go.

## No Class

When I go out with me chum
She picks lad that are scum
The ones with no class
Who grab your tits and ass

Why don't she pick someone with education
So they can hold a conversation
Not the ones who wagged school
And show you up as a rule.

Who do they think they are
Pulling and twanging her bra?
You can pick that sort every night
If all you want is shite.

## Floating

Hey, what you doing, you twat,
Piercing holes in your coke tin like that?
You think I don't know the score?
Piss off doing your shit round my door.

It used to be soap bar, gold seal, dope,
Nowadays it's anything that makes you float –
Chasing the dragon, tooting the flute –
Me, I gave them ones the boot.

Little fellas, charlies, acid and brown,
We used to think that lot were sound.
Hash, ganja, green and weed,
That's all the lot of us did need.

But when it's outside your door
I think there should be some kind of law.
At least we kept it among ourselves
And didn't force it on anyone else.

It's been hard to beat my addiction,
But we live in fact, not in fiction,
And reality is where I'd like to be
For my girl, kids, family and me.

# Part II

## Two Bullets

You haven't got a clue, you make me quite irate,
You'd want a rent rebate if you lived on my estate.

The children feed on the dreaded weed,
It used to be crack and pot, now it's the fucking lot,

They leave their evidence right outside my fence,
Then you'll hear the rumbles in this urban jungle:

It's usually someone in the lift, they've usually been left a gift,
Two bullets in their head to make sure they're dead.

## Burberry Man

The whore around the corner, Junkie Jane
Selling her crack and her bags of cocaine,
The geezer she lives with wears a Burberry hat,
He's not all that, he's a big fat twat,
He hangs round bars, smokes big cigars,
He's nothing but a pimp, he rings all the cars.

Back to Jane now, the junkie one, I mean,
Fuck me, she's back on the scene!
Scraggy as ever, eyes popping from her head,
I shout "Fuck me! I thought you were dead!"
"Any change?" is all I could hear.
"Fuck you, I ain't paying for your gear!"

It's eleven o'clock, not even midday,
And here comes Old Faithful, her junkie friend, Ray.
Up the entry they disappear,
I thought, here we go, he's selling his gear –
It was worse than that! His kecks were at his feet.
She stood there laughing, she thought it was funny,
Just a shag for a handful of money.

Here comes the fat twat, the Burberry man,
Running down the street, drinking a can.
His face is red, his belly's flopping,
Fuck me! and his eyes are popping.
"Get 'ere, you whore, you owe me dollar!"
Put that bastard in a cell, and teach him to swallow.

"Run Forrest, run!" I hear from afar,
And his mates screech up in their car.
"Get in here, and ditch the bitch,
Let's go and get a fix."

## Dirty Knicks

Why do police hang around the red light district by me?
Is it because they get sex for free
From the girls they never arrest?
Is it in their interest?

They watch the cars pull up at the kerbside
And keep quiet, because they want their ride.
They buy the girls fish and chips
To get inside their dirty knicks.

Many a vice girl goes inside that police van,
They're definitely on one hell of a scam.
It's not worth me reporting it
If a bent copper wants to dip his wick.

It's not as if it's hurting me,
Good luck to him getting sex for free.

## Annoying Shit

Why are you such a jerk?
Outside my house you lurk
Grinning when I look –
Do you want a smack?

Undies robbed off my line...
You're a dirty swine,
Out there every day:
Games you want to play?

Are you an annoying shit
Getting thrills out of it?
I've taken pictures of you
And you never knew.

I'll give them to the police,
Then this lurking will cease.

## The Whore

I'll put my foot right through your door,
I'll slap your face, you smackhead whore
The next time your pimp's in my face
For parking my car outside your place.

I'm sick of johnnies under the tree,
Always there for people to see;
Your curtains open all night long
So the kids in the street can see your thong.

You bring men back day in day out,
Then all you do is bawl and shout;
On your mobile, giving your pimp shit
Until he comes round with your hit.

He disses you in the street
And you run away in your bare feet,
All the neighbours like to get a good view –
Especially when he beats you black and blue!

Then someone will come to your aid
But it's all a put-on, you're not afraid.
You'll give as good as you get,
We've all seen it through our nets.

We felt sorry for you when you first moved in,
Never smiling, always looking grim,
But now we don't feel the same:
You're just a smackhead whore on the game.

## Dopey Joe
*(a Christmas poem)*

Dopey Joe, where did you go?
I can't see your footprints in the snow.
Metal plate in your head:
Are you dead?

Under the arches you'd sleep,
Now and then we took a peep.
With your pants around your knees:
Did you freeze?

Joe, did you go back
To the hostel with your sack?
Where the kids don't take the piss?
Better than this?

But Dopey Joe's not there
And the arches are bare
And the funny thing is some people
Don't even care.

## Kate

People blush and walk by,
Try to turn a blind eye,
They all look in disgust,
But to Kate, it's a must!
Kate sits on the step,
Legs wrapped round the dog's neck,
She's got the upper hand,
She gets muffed on demand.
If I called the RSPCA
What the hell would I say?
It's like these men that like the feel of cat's claws,
They put fish-paste all around their balls
For the cat to lick,
Are these people so sick?
The kids think it's quite neat
Having loonies on the street…

## Someone Like Me

Does your heart miss a beat
When they beat you in the street?
Does your heart ever stop racing
Cos they're gonna kick your face in?

Do you hide under the chair
You're that fucking scared?
Do you jump over the back
When you know you'll get a whack?

Where do you go for sanctuary
When you're someone like me?

## Idiots

Idiots? Who ride round in that car
Idiots? You know who you are
Idiots? Who don't use their brakes
Idiots? Who don't indicate

Idiots? Who can't even drive
Idiots? It's a wonder you're alive
Idiots? Who go too far
Idiots? Who drive that red car

Idiots? Who go beep beep beep
In the middle of the night, when you're trying to sleep

Then today we heard a big crash
Because the idiots had been on the lash
Now they don't say Idiots? any more
Because the idiots lie dead on the floor

Now it's Idiots? R. I. P.
Where you wrapped your car around that tree.

## Nappies

I'm sitting in the garden, feeling heat on me skin
When I get a whiff from me neighbour's bin,

It's full of shitty nappies, it makes you wanna barf,
And she just stands there and laughs!

I tell her it ain't no fucking joke,
That smell in your nose makes you choke,

Why they don't use the towelling ones I'll never know,
You can buy them in Boots for twenty quid a throw,

At least you could hang them out on your line –
Not leave them in the bin like that dirty swine!

## Gaff

Them gyppos over the road
In the house everyone knows;
With all the animals they keep
The place reeks.

Goats and pigs and chickens too,
Just to name a few;
They have bricks under the bed
And they nick your lead.

My dad calls them "tinkers",
Should be "stinkers",
Shit and crap everywhere,
Even on the old armchair.

I said, "Throw the chair out, you dirty gits";
Gyppo says, "That's where the dog sits."
If you wanted a good laugh
You'd go over their gaff.

## Have A Grope

My old man just got out the tub
And he's off with his mates to a lap-dancing club.
I don't mind him going, it's a bit of a crack,
And it makes him horny in the sack!
But when he says they call her fanny "Petal" –
I say, "What's it smell of, fucking metal?"
If I danced around for an hour
I know my pussy wouldn't smell like a flower,
What she got, an air freshener up her crack
What lets out a whiff when she's on her back?
He says she wriggles up the pole,
That's when they jeer, cos they see up her hole,
And if they're lucky they can pull her rope:
That's when they pay to have a grope.
Men used to pay to watch football and that,
Now they pay to see a smelly twat.

## Ga Ga

When men get the remote in their hand
They think they're the ones in command.
It's rugby on one side, football on the other –
I piss off and go to see me mother.

I go there for a tea and a chat,
It's better than watching football and that –
Though if I'm completely honest, it's not,
Mum's at the age where she's lost the fucking plot.

I listen to her music, Glen Miller and Johnny Ray,
That was music in her flipping day;
She likes me to have a waltz and do the cha cha cha,
That's when I know it's time to say ta ra.

Fuck me, after doing all that
I go back to me husband, the twat.
There he is lying on the chair;
When I walk in he just gives me a stare.

I say, "Are you coming to bed with me?"
"Not yet," he says, "I want to see Rooney's knee."
If that's what men think about at his age,
Put them all together and lock them in a cage.

## Winding Her Up

We went round town, me daughter and I
To see what bargains we could buy
But the sun was so bloody hot
The pub was about as far as we got.

I thought, why not? Weather's usually shit,
So we sat down to make the most of it;
Then we noticed the girl on the bench,
The alchie with the pissy stench.

She hangs round town most of the week,
Stands and pees in the middle of the street.
Then two women in front of us
Started annoying the alchie. How she cussed!

She might be a pisshead and a druggie too
But leave her alone, she's not annoying you.
Two seconds later the bitching had to start:
"What you looking at you stupid fucking tart?"

This middle aged woman acted all hard and that,
Making herself look like a prat;
The alchie just sat drinking cider from her bottle
Most probably wondering which one to throttle.

While the women were winding her up
She supped and supped and supped and supped
Then decided to puke everywhere!
A couple of people nearly fell off their chair.

She tipped half her bottle to get rid of the lumps,
They floated down and stopped by the stumps.
The older woman had to shout: "What you doing now?"
So the alchie says, "Shut up you silly cow."

Then all you heard was "I'll knock you out!"

And the both of 'em started to scream and shout
And as they went head to head
One of them shouts, "You're dead!"

Then as the alchie turned her back
Everyone heard a mighty WHACK –
The woman had given her a Glasgow kiss,
Didn't connect right, but a near miss.

Then the alchie threw her cider in the bin
Because she spotted the coppers coming:
They'd caught it all on CCTV
And one says to the woman, "You're coming with me."

And the alchie just walked away,
To her it was a normal day,
But to me and my daughter it was entertainment,
All of this outside the pub on the pavement.

WILLENHALL

# SCRUBBERJACK:
## 25 poems

Jackie Smallridge

*heaventree*

# SCRUBBERJACK:
## 25 poems

First edition 2007
© Jackie Smallridge 2007
Foreword © Jonathan Morley 2007

ISBN 978-1-906038-15-1

Cover photograph of 'Scrubberjack' © Ravinder
Dhaliwal 2007

Heaventree logo design by Panna Chauhan

Published in the UK by
The Heaventree Press
Koco Building,
Spon End
Coventry
CV1 3JQ

We are grateful for the financial support of

ARTS COUNCIL ENGLAND